What Can We Learn About Matter?

HOUGHTON MIFFLIN HARCOURT

matter

gas

liquid

solid

Everything is made of matter.
Matter can be a solid, liquid, or gas.

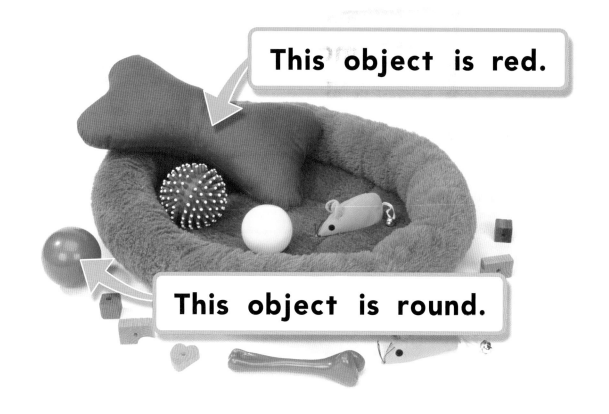

This object is red.

This object is round.

We can tell about its color and shape.

This house is light.

This house is small.

This house is heavy.

This house is big.

We can tell about its size and mass.

This object is smooth.

This object is bumpy.

When we touch objects,
we can tell how they feel.

Heat comes from the sun.

Water is liquid.

Ice is solid.

Heat changes some matter.
Heat changes ice to water.

What does heat do to matter?

The air is cool.

The water has become ice.

Cool air changes some matter.
Cool air changes water to ice.

Describe Objects

Create a chart with six columns and six rows. Label the second through sixth columns with the words *size, mass, shape, color,* and *texture.* Make copies of the chart for each child and distribute to the class. Then have children choose five objects in the classroom. Tell them to draw a picture of each object in the first column of the chart. Then have them observe each object and record its properties in the appropriate column.

Observe Heating and Cooling

Have children place a piece of ice outside on a warm day. Ask them to observe what happens to the ice. Have children draw before-and-after pictures to show how heat changed the ice. Ask partners to discuss their pictures.

Vocabulary

cool   matter

heat